What Is the BIBLE?

WRITTEN BY **Rachel Held Evans**
and **Matthew Paul Turner**

ILLUSTRATED BY **Ying Hui Tan**

CONVERGENT

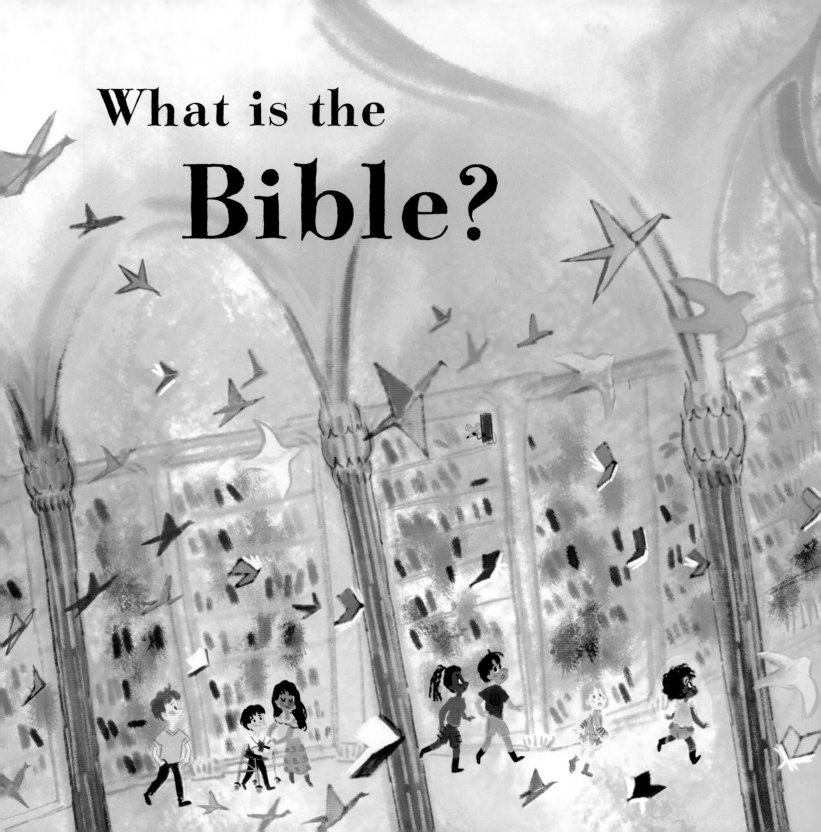

What is the
Bible?

It's a big book that's filled with all kinds of stories.

Some of the stories are scary. Some are funny. Some are strange and mysterious.

And some of them are beautiful, the kind that will fill you up with wonder and hope.

Now, imagine if **God** put all those stories in one place.

That's what the Bible is, a huge **library** you can hold in your hands.

Many of the stories in the
Bible are about God.

The very first one is about
God **creating** the universe.
And creating you and me.

There are **stories** about God
wrestling, about God ruling,
and about God providing.

But not all the stories are about God.

There are stories about **monsters.**

There are huge dragons with scaly tails,
giants with sharp swords, and a king
who turned into a beast for seven years.

There are stories about **animals.**

There is a crafty snake that tempts people with power, a donkey that sees an angel and speaks aloud, and a big fish that swallows a man whole.

There are helpful ravens, soaring eagles, humble sparrows, and a lost sheep that eventually gets **found.**

There are stories about **people** too.

There are powerful people,
brave people, proud people,
terrible people, and faithful people.

The Bible tells us about good kings and bad kings, kind queens and mean queens. There are stories about warriors who do great things and warriors who make choices that are ugly and violent. And there are stories about regular people who become **strong and brave.**

There are people who **survive** fiery furnaces, dens filled with lions, and terrible plagues involving slimy frogs, creepy crawly insects, and enormous hail.

We learn about people who call fire down from the sky and people who predict the future from their **dreams.**

The Bible is filled with **magical moments,** like food falling from the sky, water bursting out of rocks, and bushes that become consumed by fire but don't ever burn up.

There are unbelievable events and **miraculous experiences.**

A large body of water splits in two,
a rainstorm lasts forty days and nights
and floods the entire planet, and the
sun stands still on a certain day.

Not every story in the Bible
is told the same way.

There are poems and songs, wise sayings and letters, and memories that someone wrote down so they **would not forget.**

The **poems** are about love
and mercy, bravery and
distress, colorful celebrations
and sad disappointments.

The **songs** tell us that God is always near, that God is for us and not against us, and that God is our shepherd, our protector, our healer.

The **wise sayings** often give us ideas for how to live with passion and purpose, how to get along with others, and how to make peace with people who have hurt us.

The **letters** hold words of encouragement,
words of hope, and words of affirmation
for a life well lived.

But the best part of all?

In the Bible we meet **Jesus,**
who teaches us new things about
God, faith, and ourselves.

Jesus tells us **we are light.**

Jesus tells us **we are welcome.**

Jesus tells us **we love God when we love people.**

Jesus tells us to care for people who are
sick, to feed people who are hungry, and
to use our gifts to make the world better.

Jesus tells us that
God loves each one of us.

What is the
Bible?

It's God's library of stories told
in many different ways.

And if a story in that library is confusing or scary or sad, we can imagine how Jesus, **who loves us,** might tell us that story.

The Bible can help us **heal**.

It can make us **think.**

It can **bring** us together.

It can **remind** us why we're here.

It can show us
the way home.

Hardback IBSN 978-0-593-19333-4
Ebook IBSN 978-0-593-19334-1

The Library of Congress catalog record is available
 at https://lccn.loc.gov/2024023479.

Printed in China

convergentbooks.com

987654321

First Edition

Cover design by Zaiah Sampson

Book design by Zaiah Sampson
based on design by Sonia Persad